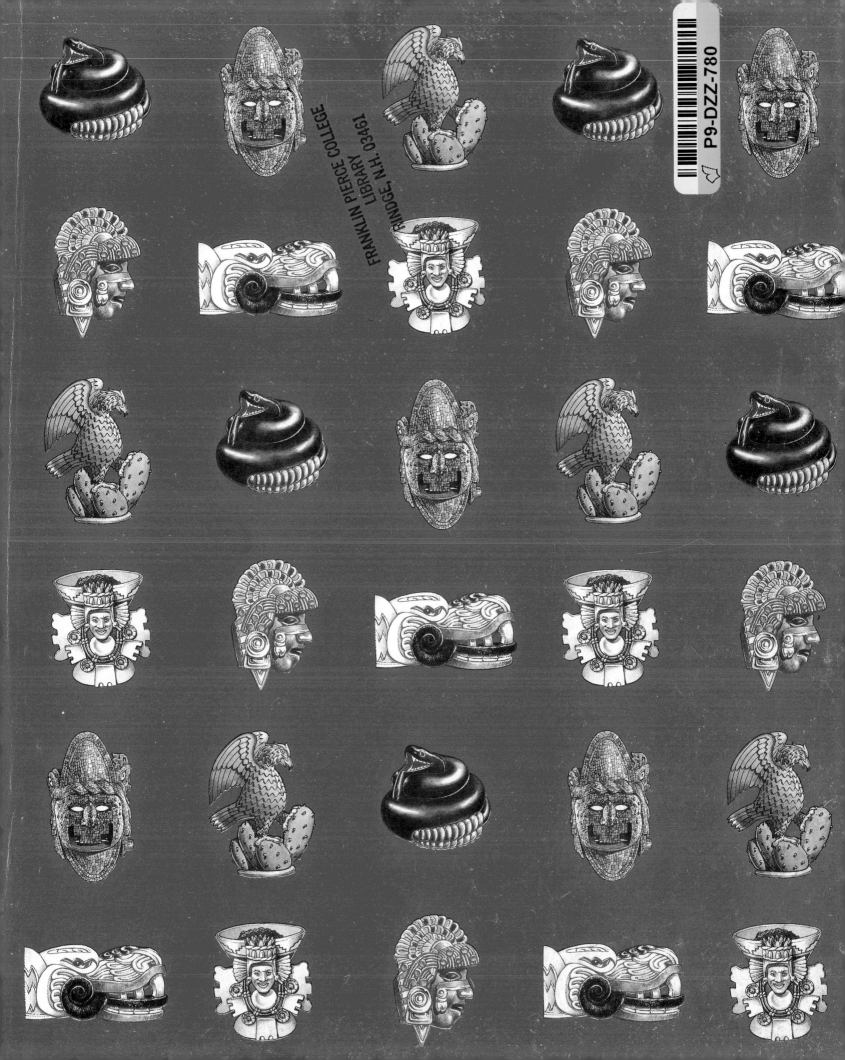

THE AZTECS

TIM WOOD

Viking

Acknowledgements

The publishers would like to thank Dr Elizabeth Baquedano for her invaluable assistance and advice during the preparation of this book; Bill Le Fever, who illustrated the see-through pages and jacket; and the organizations which have given their permission to reproduce the following pictures:

Ancient Art & Architecture: 18, 40 (bottom centre)
Biblioteca Medicea Laurenziana, Florence: 13 (from the Florentine Codex)
Bodleian Library, Oxford: 10, 21, 23, 34, 35, 39 (all from the Codex Mendoza)
British Museum (Museum of Mankind): 22
British Library: 42 (top right), 42 (bottom), 44 (from the Lienzo de Tlaxcalla)
Mary Evans Picture Library: 43 (Aztec manuscript drawing)
Werner Forman Archive: 6, 7 (bottom), 9 , 12, 19 (top), 24, 28 (top left), 29 (bottom), 30, 32 (top left), 32 (top right), 38 (bottom), 40 (bottom left), 40 (bottom right)
Robert Frerck, Susan Griggs Agency: 28 (centre), 36,
Hamlyn Children's Books: 26-27
Nick Saunders, Barbara Heller Photos: 16
Michael Holford: 5, 38 (top)
Museum für Völkerkunde, Vienna: 19 (bottom), 29 (top)
Spectrum Colour Library: 15
ZEFA: 7 (top)

Illustrators:
Philip Hood: 8-9, 11, 12, 13, 14, 15, 16, 18-19, 20, 21, 22, 23, 24, 27, 28. 30 (top right), 30-31, 32, 34, 35, 37, 38, 39, 40, 44-45
Richard Hook: 29, 46-47
Bill Le Fever: 17, 25, 33, 41
Maltings Partnership: 16 (top left)
Roger Stewart: 4-5, 6-7, 8 (top left), 10 (top left), 20 (top left), 26 (top left), 27 (bottom right), 34 (top left), 37 (top right), 40 (top left), 42 (top left), 45 (bottom right)

Editor: Andrew Farrow
Series Designer: Nick Leggett
Picture Researcher: Judy Todd
Production Controller: Linda Spillane

VIKING
Published by the Penguin Group
Viking Penguin, a division of Penguin Books USA Inc.,
375 Hudson Street, New York, New York 10014, U.S.A.
Penguin Books Ltd, 27 Wrights Lane, London W8 5TZ, England
Penguin Books Australia Ltd, Ringwood, Victoria, Australia
Penguin Books Canada Ltd, 10 Alcorn Avenue, Toronto, Ontario, Canada M4V 3B2
Penguin Books (N.Z.) Ltd, 182-190 Wairau Road, Auckland 10, New Zealand
Penguin Books Ltd, Registered Offices: Harmondsworth, Middlesex, England
First published in 1992 by Viking Penguin, a division of Penguin Books USA Inc.

1 3 5 7 9 10 8 6 4 2

Library of Congress catalog card number: 91-68542
ISBN 0-670-84492-6
Printed in Belgium

Books printed and bound by Proost, Belgium

CONTENTS

THE AZTECS OF MEXICO

North America

South America

HUASTECS

CHICHIMECS

GULF OF MEXICO

TARASCANS

* Tula

(TOLTECS)

* Teotihuacan

Tenochtitlan *

Popocatepetl

Malinalco *

¤ * Tlaxcala

* Veracruz

TLAXCALANS

Huaxtapec *

* Cholula

(OLMECS)

PACIFIC OCEAN

River Balsas

San Lorenzo *

MIXTECS

(ZAPOTECS)

Key to main map
MIXTECS
Independent nations
(ZAPOTECS)
Pre-Aztec peoples
* *Cities*
¤ *Volcano*

The Aztec Empire covered roughly the same area as modern Mexico. Its magnificent capital city, Tenochtitlan, was built in the Valley of Mexico, on islands in Lake Texcoco, the same site where Mexico City, the capital of Mexico, stands today.

Before 1519, Europeans knew almost nothing about the continent of America. In that year a small band of Spanish adventurers led by Hernan Cortes landed in Mexico. To their amazement, they discovered a great civilization which stretched between the Atlantic and Pacific coasts.

THE AZTEC EMPIRE
This civilization contained about 15 million people who lived in nearly 500 towns and cities. Some of the cities were larger and better organized than any European city of the time. The people belonged to many different groups, each of which had its own lands and traditions.

They were citizens of an enormous Empire which was ruled by the most powerful of all the groups - the Aztecs.

THE LAND OF MEXICO
When Cortes was asked by King Charles V of Spain to describe Mexico, he crumpled up a sheet of paper and tossed it on the table before the monarch. The paper represented the landscape of Mexico, a place covered with mountains and rough crags. Only narrow strips along the coasts and in the Yucatan Peninsula are flat lowlands.

Much of Mexico is very hot and scorched by the sun. The land is often barren, too rocky or salt-soaked to allow any plants other than scrubby trees and grasses to grow. One of the few places with fertile soil is the Valley of Mexico, which is over 2,000 yards (meters) above sea level. This valley was the center of the Aztec Empire.

CRUEL LAND

Mexico is frequently struck by natural disasters. Drought, earthquakes, and volcanoes can scar the land. One of the largest volcanoes was called Popacatapetl by the Aztecs, which means "Smoking Mountain."

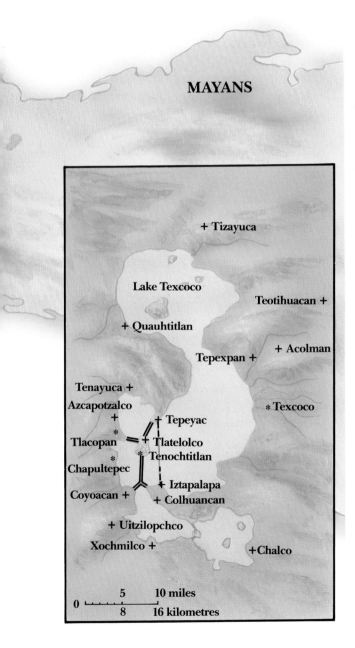

MAYANS

Lake Texcoco

+ Tizayuca

Teotihuacan +

+ Quauhtitlan

Tepexpan +

+ Acolman

Tenayuca +

Azcapotzalco
+

* Texcoco

† Tepeyac

Tlacopan *
† Tlatelolco
* Tenochtitlan

Chapultepec *

+ Iztapalapa

Coyoacan +
+ Colhuancan

+ Uitzilopchco

Xochmilco +
+ Chalco

5	10 miles
0	
8	16 kilometres

CRUEL GODS

This harsh land bred tough people. They worshipped demanding gods whom they believed controlled nature. These powerful gods could bring flood, famine, and earthquake and had to be given gifts to keep them happy. The most valuable gift the Aztecs had to offer was life itself. Only by sacrificing human beings, and offering their hearts to the gods, could the sun be made to rise, the rain to fall, and the crops to grow.

As Aztec civilization grew in importance, so human sacrifice became more important, too. By the time the Spanish arrived, the Aztecs were sacrificing about 20,000 people each year. Since most of the victims were prisoners taken in battle, the Aztecs believed that war was essential if their Empire was to survive. To the Spanish outsiders, Aztec life appeared to be a mad, bloody pattern of continual war and gruesome ceremonies.

In spite of their bloodthirsty religion, the Aztecs were not simple savages. Among their many achievements were great feats of engineering using only the simplest tools; organizing the lives and work of hundreds of thousands of people; and the writing of beautiful poetry.

MYSTERIOUS LEGEND

The Aztecs had unshakeable faith in their own legends and prophecies. One of their legends predicted that in 1519 there would be a conflict between two of their gods. One of these was Tezcatlipoca, the "Smoking Mirror," god of war and the special god of the Aztecs; the other was Quetzalcoatl, the "Feathered Serpent," a pale-skinned god with great powers who would come from the east and claim the Empire for himself. In a final battle between these two gods, the Aztec Empire would be utterly destroyed. This, the last and most terrible Aztec prophecy, was to prove the most truthful and accurate of all their beliefs.

The center of the Aztec Empire was at Tenochtitlan and the cities surrounding Lake Texcoco.

Key: *Cities of Triple Alliance* + *Other towns*
= *Causeways* --- *Dyke*

A mask which probably is meant to represent the face of one of the most important of all the Aztec gods - Tezcatlipoca, or "Smoking Mirror." The mask is made of small squares of the semi-precious stones lignum and turquoise. These are laid in the form of a mosaic over an actual human skull, complete with some of its original teeth!

THE FIRST CIVILIZATIONS

This colossal stone head was carved by Olmec sculptors. It probably represents a ruler of San Lorenzo, one of the oldest Olmec cities. The head weighs over 20 tons and was brought to the site by raft, along the coast, and then dragged overland.

The first people probably came to America from Asia about 50,000 years ago. They moved across what is now the Bering Straits over the land-bridge which then connected the two continents. It took thousands of years for their descendants to spread throughout the rest of the American continent.

THE FIRST MEXICANS

The first Americans lived in small groups, hunting wild game and gathering seeds, fruit, and nuts. Gradually they moved southwards until, about 10,000 years ago, groups of people living in what is now the Valley of Mexico discovered how to grow their own food. Their main crops were maize and squash.

By about 3000 BC, these first Mexicans were living in farming settlements. They also discovered how to make pots and to weave cloth. Some archaeological evidence suggests that they practiced human sacrifice and cannibalism.

THE OLMECS

About 1200 BC, a civilization was created by a group called the Olmecs, who lived in the jungles along the eastern coast. They built ceremonial centers, with stone pyramids, palaces, and statues, and they had a well-developed religion based on worship of the jaguar. The Olmecs knew about mathematics and astronomy. They traded with the Mayans who lived to the east, and with people who later became known as the Zapotecs and Mixtecs.

THE CITY OF TEOTIHUACAN

Between AD 300 and 750, a new group gained control of the Valley of Mexico. They built as their capital a magnificent stone city, called Teotihuacan, or "Place of the Gods," which contained gigantic pyramids and broad avenues.

Much of the Aztecs' culture and their way of life was based on the civilizations which had come before them. The Teotihuacans built a magnificent city and worshipped many deities, particularly Quetzalcoatl and Tlaloc. Their main pyramids were the temples of the sun and the moon.

The Teotihuacan empire flourished for two centuries, growing rich through trade. But the city was demolished, either by conquest or by the Teotihuacans themselves during a time of famine and revolts. Most of the houses were destroyed by fire and the city became deserted apart from a few people who lived among the ruins.

Teotihuacans. Just before 1200, Tula was attacked and destroyed, probably by a tribe from the north called the Chichimecs, or "Dog People," who were said to eat raw meat and wear animal skins.

THE AZTECS

The last tribe to enter the Valley of Mexico were the Mexicas or Tenochcas. They were a poor wandering tribe who spoke Nahuatl, a language which had been used by the Toltecs. We know these people as Aztecs. They were outcasts, with nowhere to live. They lived on whatever land they could find until they were driven away by other local tribes. Finally they took refuge on a swampy island in Lake Texcoco, the only land in the Valley of Mexico which was not settled by another tribe. At some time between 1325 and 1345 they built a village. This village grew slowly until eventually it became the magnificent capital city of the Aztec Empire.

THE TOLTECS

About AD 1000 to 1150, a people called the Toltecs controlled a large empire in Mexico. They built pyramids and sacred ball-courts in their capital, Tula. They were a fierce, warlike people whose army contained crack soldiers called Eagle and Jaguar knights. The Toltecs practiced human sacrifice and worshipped many of the same gods as the Olmecs and

The Mixtecs were expert goldsmiths. This gold ornament, shaped like a bearded god, was fastened to the wearer's nose!

THE RISE OF THE AZTECS

The eagle and cactus, the sign from Huitzilopochtli which showed the Aztecs where to build their city. The eagle symbol appears on the flag and coat of arms of the modern Republic of Mexico.

According to their own legends the Aztecs lived originally on Aztlan, an island in a lake. They came to the shore in their canoes and found a statue of their god Huitzilopochtli. Their god told them to travel to a new land, taking with them a number of other tribes.

THE AZTECS' JOURNEY

During their wanderings, some of these other tribes left the Aztecs and settled down. The Aztecs continued their journey until they reached the Valley of Mexico, where they found all the best land occupied by other tribes. Their god gave them a sign, an eagle sitting on a cactus while it ate a snake, to show them where to build their village. They called it Tenochtitlan, which meant "Place of the Cactus."

THE POVERTY OF THE AZTECS

These settlers probably lived in mud and reed huts, and caught wild fowl, frogs, and fish. They had no wood and so had to trade with the tribes on the mainland for materials to build their first real houses. They also had to pay tribute to the powerful Tepanecs who controlled most of the shore, so they hardly had enough food to stay alive.

I have no joy, I have no gladness;
The earth does not fill me.
I have suffered sorrows in the world. The earth has only been lent to us. Tomorrow, or the day after, The giver of life will beckon us to his home.

—— *Aztec poem* ——

The Aztecs used canoes for travelling around the lake, and for carrying all kinds of cargoes, from gold dust to human dung. The lake waters provided them with fish, which they caught with spears, and wildfowl, which they caught with nets.

8

TENOCHTITLAN GROWS

At first, the richer tribes around the lake despised the Aztecs. But, gradually, the Aztecs began to prosper. They learned how to make reed rafts which they anchored in the marshes to form floating gardens, called *chinampas*. The rich mud from the lake was used as soil and produced large harvests. They filled in the spaces between the *chinampas* to make more room for houses. They built causeways to the mainland and to other islands, to make travelling easier. Gradually the original swampy island was transformed into a busy, prosperous town. The Aztecs also began to spread to other islands and build on them.

CONQUEST

Few people, except perhaps the priests, could have foreseen that a great Empire would develop from such beginnings. Finally, in about 1426 the Aztecs joined with the people of other lakeside cities, such as Tlateloco, Tlacopan, and Texcoco, to defeat the Tepanecs. The Tepanec land was shared out between the victorious cities. Now the Aztecs had a foothold on the mainland. The Aztec capital Tenochtitlan, and Texcoco and Tlacopan, formed a powerful "Triple Alliance," which began to conquer scores of other cities in the Valley of Mexico.

Aztec picture writing showing the journey from their original home known as Aztlan. The glyph, or picture writing, for the date (One Flint) appears in the center. The footprints show movement.

MONTEZUMA I

This conquest accelerated under Montezuma I (1440-68), whose armies defeated the Mixtecs and the tribes to the east. Other Aztec Emperors, such as Axayacatl and Montezuma II, continued these victories. Tenochtitlan became the most powerful city in Mexico as Tlacopan and Texcoco fell more under the control of the Aztecs. It seemed as if nothing could stop the expansion of the Aztec Empire. Then, in 1519, news arrived in Tenochtitlan that white men in boats as big as mountains had arrived at the coast. Within two years, the Aztec Empire would be utterly destroyed.

An ornamental featherwork disc showing the whirlpool symbols of Chalchihuitlicue, the goddess of water. The Aztecs were very skilled at featherwork.

9

THE AZTEC EMPIRE

The Aztec glyph for the god Huitzilopochtli. Witnesses in court had to swear by Huitzilopochtli to tell the truth, so if they were caught in a lie, they could be put to death for a crime against the god.

An Aztec lawcourt. Four judges, with their junior helpers behind them, sit on the left wearing their official headdresses. Six criminals - three men and three women - sit on the right.

In 1519, the Aztec Empire stretched across Mexico from the Atlantic to the Pacific. It contained nearly 500 towns and was divided into 38 provinces. The people who lived in the Empire came from many groups. Most of the people who lived in the Empire were not Aztecs, although they were subject to Aztec rule.

CONTROLLING THE EMPIRE

The Aztecs were not interested in organizing the everyday lives of the towns and cities they conquered. They wanted only three things from them. The first was that all the people within the Empire should worship the Aztec god Huitzilopochtli, as well as their own tribal gods. Secondly, each city had to send taxes, called tribute, to Tenochtitlan. The third requirement was that each city had to be loyal and obedient to the Aztecs, particularly by supplying soldiers in time of war.

CONQUEST

Most of the cities within the Empire hated paying tribute to the Aztecs. But there was very little they could do about it. When the Aztecs conquered a city, they usually captured thousands of prisoners, mostly young men. With their best warriors taken to Tenochtitlan to be sacrificed, the conquered cities had no way to challenge the powerful Aztec armies.

And when we saw all those cities and villages built in the water... and that straight and level causeway leading to Mexico, we were astounded. Some of our soldiers asked whether it was... a dream.

— *Bernal Diaz* —

ENEMIES OF THE AZTECS

There were several groups which were never conquered by the Aztecs. The Tarascans, who lived to the west, drove back an invasion by the Aztec king, Axayacatl. Much closer to Tenochtitlan, the powerful Tlaxcalans became the allies of the Spanish invaders and played an important part in the overthrow of the hated Aztecs.

LAWS

Aztec law covered almost every aspect of life, including criminal behavior, divorce, and ownership of land. No single list of laws covered the entire Empire, so laws varied from place to place.

Many laws were designed to protect the class system. It was forbidden, for example, for an ordinary person to wear the cotton clothes of a noble. Other laws protected people's livelihoods. Stealing crops, for example, was a serious crime. Drunkenness was a very serious crime, except in the case of old people, who were seldom punished.

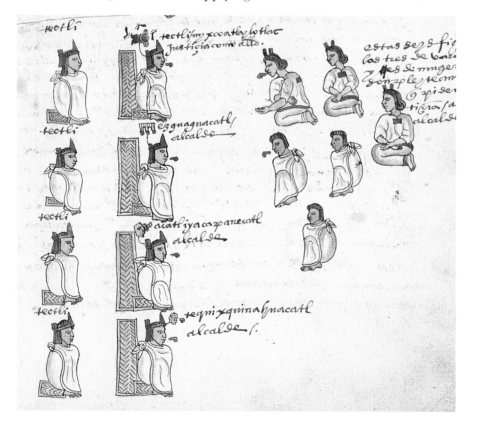

LAW COURTS

Minor cases were dealt with by local courts, with senior warriors acting as judges. More serious cases were sent to Tenochtitlan to be tried in front of the *teccalco* court, which was run by experienced judges. The most serious cases, and those which involved nobles, were heard by even more senior courts which sat in the Emperor's palace. In one of them the Emperor himself was the chief judge.

PUNISHMENTS

The Aztecs had no system of imprisonment. Punishment fell into two categories. For minor crimes, the lawbreaker was required to repay the injured party in goods or work. If a fight broke out, the person judged guilty of starting it would have to pay for medical treatment and anything which had been damaged. The criminal could also be made a slave of the injured party until he had worked off twice the value of any property.

Major crimes, such as murder, stealing from the market, highway robbery, or being drunk in public, could be punished by death. The criminal could be sent to the altar, or stoned to death on the spot. First offenders often received lighter punishments, such as having their head shaved or having their house knocked down. The nobles, who were supposed to set a good example, received much harsher punishments than ordinary people.

The causeways were the lifeline of Tenochtitlan, the heart of the Empire. They thronged with messengers bringing news from distant parts of the Empire, farmers coming to market, and merchants setting out on and returning from trading missions.

11

THE AZTEC PEOPLE

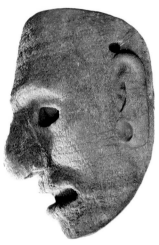

A stone mask in an unusually realistic and natural style, shows the head of an Aztec nobleman.

Aztecs were short, stocky people. They probably all had black hair and dark eyes. The different social classes of Aztecs were distinguished by the richness of their clothes and by their haircuts. Men were generally beardless, while women wore yellow face powder. During festivals and for ceremonial occasions, the men painted their faces and bodies.

THE EMPEROR

The leader of the Aztecs was the Emperor. He rarely appeared in public, and was treated like a god. When an Emperor died, his successor was chosen from the royal family by a small group of nobles and priests, usually for his experience and bravery in war.

Aztec healers, ticitls, *knew how to cure many illnesses. Some of their medicines, which were mostly made from herbs and other plants, were surprisingly effective.*

THE EMPEROR'S ADVISERS

The Emperor's chief adviser was a man who had the strange title of Cihuacoatl or "Snake Woman." The Snake Woman was the deputy emperor, chief judge, and the person who dealt with the day-to-day running of the Empire. Beneath the Snake Woman were four generals who commanded the soldiers from the four districts of Tenochtitlan. Under them was the council, a group of advisers to the Emperor.

THE NOBLES

Below the rulers were the great nobles, the *tlatoani,* who governed the provinces. Below them were the lesser nobles, the *tecuhtlis,* officials who controlled the daily life in the cities, and the judges and generals.

Nobles were usually quite rich. They received gifts of land in newly conquered areas from the Emperor and did not have to pay taxes. Ordinary people could become nobles by showing skill and courage in battle, but most nobles inherited their titles and land.

THE PEOPLE

Most of the population were ordinary tribespeople, the *maceualtin* or "common people." They were divided into family groups or clans, called *calpulli.* Each *calpulli* had a certain amount of land to farm, which was divided up among the members of the clan by a council that met once a year. Some ordinary people had so much land that they were richer than some of the nobles.

SLAVES

The lowest group in Aztec society were the slaves. Some were prisoners taken in battle, others were Aztecs who had fallen on hard times. Citizens of Tenochtitlan could be sold into slavery if they had large debts, or if they were caught stealing. Some even sold themselves into slavery to get food and shelter when their own crops failed.

Slaves were usually well treated but they could be sacrificed if three owners had been forced to sell them because they had behaved badly. Some of the slaves farmed the land owned by the nobles, and others were household servants.

THE SLAVE MARKET

Slaves were bought and sold at slave markets, the largest of which was in the city of Azcapotzalco. Slaves were paraded in fine clothes to look their best. As soon as they were sold, the fine clothes were stripped off and they were put in wooden cages to await their new owners. After the sale, slaves had one final chance to regain their freedom. If they could escape from the marketplace and reach the ruler's palace, they were freed. No one except the new owner or his son was allowed to catch an escaping slave, and people who tried to do so could themselves be made into slaves.

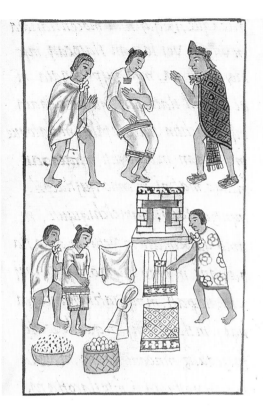

Once a year, and more often in times of famine, the Emperor distributed gifts of cloaks and food to the poor people of Tenochtitlan. The goods were part of the vast amounts of tribute sent from conquered cities and stored in the Emperor's palace.

Slaves were often sold in the city marketplaces like ordinary goods. Some slaves, especially lazy and aggressive ones, and those who were thieves, wore wooden yokes to make escape more difficult.

TENOCHTITLAN

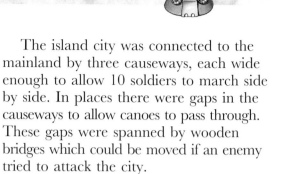

When the Spanish reached the Valley of Mexico in 1519, they were amazed at what they saw. Here, at Lake Texcoco, was the heart of the Aztec Empire. Dozens of small towns and villages clung to the shore, and the waters thronged with canoes. On a large island stood the magnificent Aztec capital, Tenochtitlan. Its giant stone temples and large houses seemed to rise out of the surface of the water.

THE CAUSEWAYS

The Aztecs had greatly expanded their original muddy island by driving thousands of wooden stakes into the bed of the lake to make strong foundations. Rocks and earth had been laid to make a level surface on which to build the city.

The island city was connected to the mainland by three causeways, each wide enough to allow 10 soldiers to march side by side. In places there were gaps in the causeways to allow canoes to pass through. These gaps were spanned by wooden bridges which could be moved if an enemy tried to attack the city.

THE WATER SUPPLY

Fresh water was brought to the city by of two aqueducts. Each aqueduct carried two pipes, so that one could always be used if the other was being cleaned or repaired. The water went to public fountains and reservoirs which were placed throughout the city. To the east of the city the Aztecs had built a 16-mile-long dyke. This was pierced with sluice gates which controlled the level of the lake in times of

Every conceivable product was sold at Tenochtitlan's markets, from building materials to worms to eat. The most colorful part was where birds and feathers were sold. Trade was by mainly by barter because the Aztecs had no real system of coinage, although they did use cacao beans and quills filled with gold dust as money.

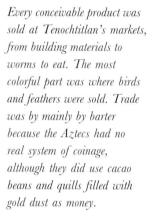

flood, and stopped salty water from eastern parts of the lake polluting the fresh water around Tenochtitlan.

The city was laid out in a grid pattern, divided by canals which acted as "roads" for the canoe traffic, and wide, paved avenues which met at the central Temple Precinct. All the streets were spotlessly clean. They were swept and sprinkled with water regularly. There were public bathrooms, and waste was collected from them every day, loaded into large canoes, and taken to be spread on the fields as fertilizer.

On reaching the market-place... we were astounded at the great number of people and the quantities of merchandise, and at the orderliness and good arrangements that prevailed... Every kind of merchandise... had its fixed place marked for it.

— Bernal Diaz —

MARKETS

At least 100,000 people lived in the city, more than twice the population of any European city at that time. The city was divided into four districts, each with its own temples, schools, and markets. At the edges of the city were floating gardens, and the simple, single-story houses of the poorer people. Nearer the heart of the city were the grander houses of the more important citizens. In the center was the great square with the Temple Precinct, main market, and Montezuma's palace.

The markets were held every five days. People came from miles around to buy and sell goods, and to exchange news and gossip. The market squares were divided into several sections where different goods were displayed. Every imaginable item was sold, including food, clothing, skins, weapons edged with obsidian (a black flint-like volcanic glass), copper axes, canoes, herbs, and quills of gold dust. Officials patrolled the market, checking that stall-holders had paid their fees, inspecting the quality of the goods, and making sure that prices were not too high. Thieves or cheats were tried on the spot by twelve judges - they could be beaten to death for their crimes.

Every city had its ritual ball-court where players wearing protective padding tried to knock a heavy rubber ball through stone hoops. Many ball-courts were richly decorated with friezes (left).

This stone stood at the base of the Great Temple. It was over 3 yards in diameter and shows the goddess Coyolxauqui. Aztec legend tells how she was killed by Huitzilopochtli and her head thrown into the sky to become the golden moon.

During one four-day ceremony at least 20,000 people were sacrificed. Their bodies lay in heaps round the base of the Great Temple and the steps became slippery with blood.

The Great Temple was the main religious building in Tenochtitlan. It was here that the Aztecs carried out their most terrible ceremonies of human sacrifice. During great festivals, hundreds, sometimes thousands, of prisoners lined up on the steps. They shuffled slowly upwards toward one of the great altars which stood on the top, in front of the shrines.

BLOODY SACRIFICES

When victims reached the altar, they were seized by the priests and stretched across the sacrificial stone. A priest with an obsidian knife slashed open each chest and tore out the victim's heart. The heart was placed in a bowl or the *chacmool* - a stone statue in the shape of a lying man in front of Tlaloc's shrine. The heart was the food of the Aztec gods who kept the world and the sun alive.

The Great Temple, a huge four-tiered pyramid, towered over the city. It was built from huge blocks of stone, carried down from the mountains, and was decorated with paintings and carvings. Twin staircases led to the summit, about 30 yards (meters) above the ground.

The chacmool *was probably meant to be a messenger who took the offerings of hearts to the gods.*

HOLY SHRINES

On the commanding heights of the Great Temple pyramid stood twin shrines, the left-hand one dedicated to Tlaloc, the god of rain and fertility, and the other to Huitzilopochtli, or "Blue Hummingbird," god of the sun and war. These gods represented the Aztecs' two main concerns in life - rain, which was vital for good harvests, and war, which provided a steady stream of prisoners for sacrifice.

> **Here too all was covered with blood, both walls and altar... In that small platform were large knives and many hearts that had been burned... the stench here was like a slaughter-house, and we could scarcely stay in the place.**
>
> —— *Bernal Diaz* ——

The two shrines were decorated with richly carved wood and paintings of grotesque creatures. Inside were giant statues of the gods. The figure of Tlaloc was half human and half alligator. His body was covered with seeds to represent the fertility of the land. The figure of Huitzilopochtli was covered with precious stones, gold, and pearls. His eyes were mirrors staring out of a golden mask. A necklace of golden human hearts hung around his neck.

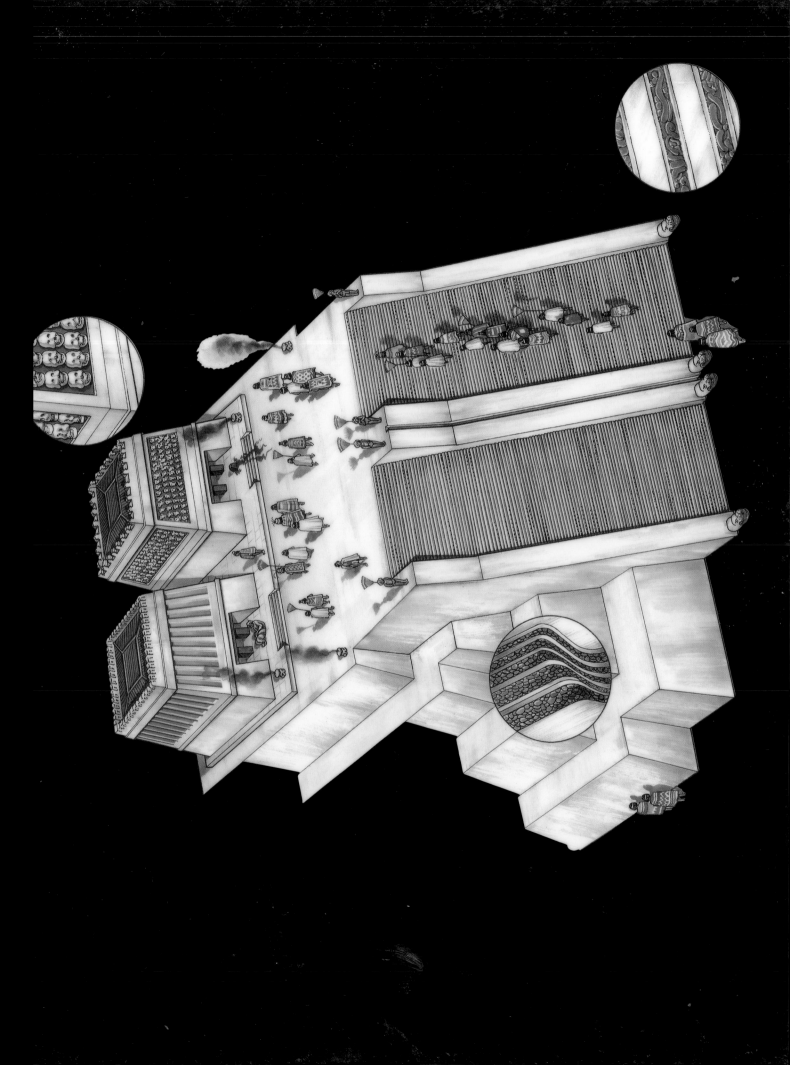

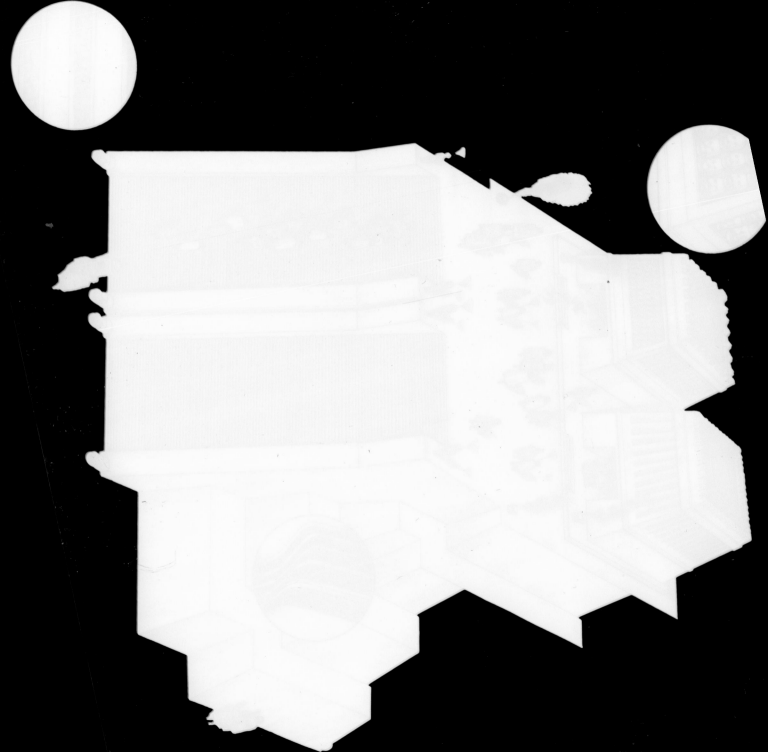

THE GREAT TEMPLE OF TENOCHTITLAN

1 **Shrine of Huitzilopochtli**
2 **Shrine of Tlaloc**
3 **The *chacmool***
4 **Remains of second Great Temple**
5 **Brazier for burning incense**
6 **Rubble between temples**
7 **Stone serpent heads**
8 **Sacrificial stone**
9 **Coyolxauhqui stone**
10 **Earlier remains**

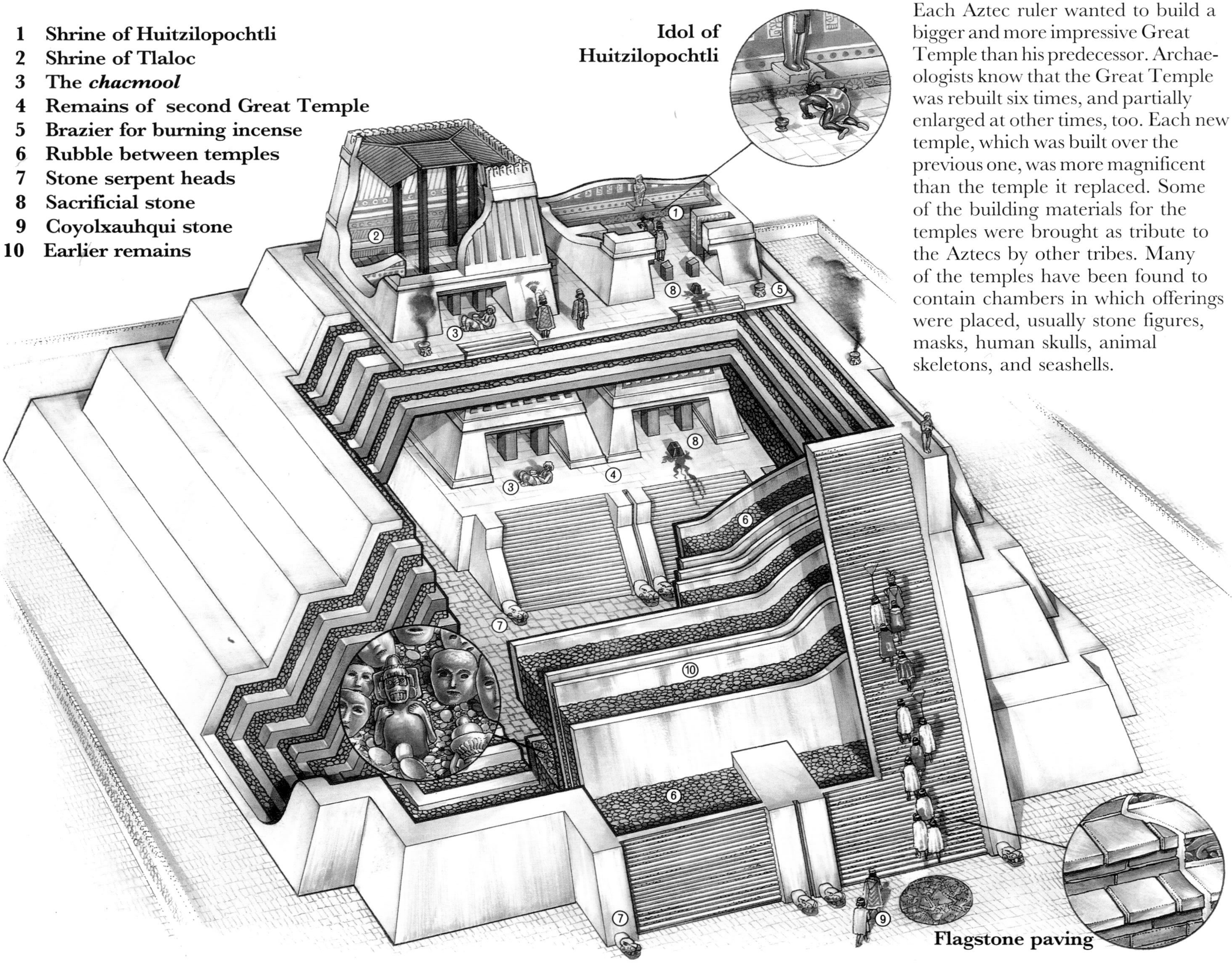

The seven Great Temples

Each Aztec ruler wanted to build a bigger and more impressive Great Temple than his predecessor. Archaeologists know that the Great Temple was rebuilt six times, and partially enlarged at other times, too. Each new temple, which was built over the previous one, was more magnificent than the temple it replaced. Some of the building materials for the temples were brought as tribute to the Aztecs by other tribes. Many of the temples have been found to contain chambers in which offerings were placed, usually stone figures, masks, human skulls, animal skeletons, and seashells.

Idol of Huitzilopochtli

Flagstone paving

THE AZTEC ARMY

A carving of an Eagle knight, one of the elite soldiers.

The Jaguar and Eagle knights wore helmets shaped like the heads of the animals whose names they had taken. The Jaguar knights dressed in ocelot skins, while the Eagle knights wore feathered suits.

The army was vital to the survival of the Aztec Empire. Serving bravely as a soldier could save an Aztec from poverty, while the booty from conquered lands and peoples brought prosperity to the Empire. The Aztecs used, and provoked, any excuse to start a war.

THE COMMANDERS

The Emperor was commander-in-chief of the Aztec army. Each city under his control had, when requested, to send soldiers to fight. As a result he could raise an army of over 100,000 warriors for a campaign. The Aztecs often overwhelmed their enemies by sheer force of numbers.

The warriors fought in city groups, led by their own officers, but under the Emperor's overall command. Emperors either led their armies in person, or sent their most trusted relations as commanders.

THE OFFICERS

The officers were usually knights. They were full-time soldiers who were picked from the best warriors at an early age. There were three main orders of knights - the Arrow, Eagle, and Jaguar knights. Important officers had large feather banners fastened to their backs by a harness, leaving their hands free to fight.

THE WARRIORS

Every able-bodied Aztec man was expected to leave the fields and fight when the great war drum sounded. Boys were all trained at school to handle weapons. Once they reached the age of 15, they could be called upon to go to war. Most were glad to fight, because success in battle was one of the few ways in which poor Aztecs could become rich and famous. If they died in battle, their families would be compensated, while their spirits went to a special heaven near the sun.

Warriors were not paid, but those who

18

A warrior in quilted armor uses a spear thrower. The spear was slotted into a groove, with its butt trapped by a small hook. When the spear thrower was swung forward, it extended the arm of the warrior, allowing him to fling the spear at greater speed.

distinguished themselves in battle were often rewarded with gifts of land, slaves, and clothing. Any warrior who captured four prisoners was made into a nobleman. Those wounded in battle won the right to wear a long cloak of honor to hide their scars. On the other hand, those who showed cowardice could be stoned to death.

WEAPONS

Aztec weapons were kept in the *tlacochcalco*, or arsenal, and were only handed out when the signal for war was given. The warriors used slings, bows, and bone- or obsidian-tipped arrows. They also carried long spears which were thrown by means of a wooden spear thrower, called an *atlatl*. The favorite Aztec weapon for close-quarter fighting was a cross between a club and a sword, called a *maquahuitl*. It was about a yard (meter) long and had razor-sharp obsidian blades fixed around the edges. It was said by the Spanish that a single blow from one of these swords could cut the head off a horse.

ARMOR

Although the Aztec army didn't have an official uniform, most of the warriors wore suits of quilted cotton soaked in salt water to make them stiff. There was a vertical opening down the back, fastened by lacing. These suits, which were very effective armor, and able to stop an arrow or javelin, were often decorated with feathers and paint. Many warriors wore bright feathered head-dresses and carried wicker shields which were covered in leather and decorated with feathers.

A warrior's spear thrower, showing the groove into which the spear was slotted. The hook at the top of the groove was inserted into the butt of the spear handle. This one is covered with gold and carved with scenes.

This beautiful Aztec shield, which is decorated with feathers, was given to Cortes as a gift by Montezuma.

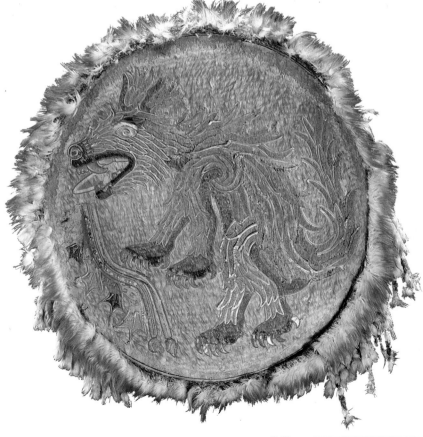

WARFARE

The Aztec glyph for a defeated city was a picture showing the destruction of the temple which inevitably followed the conquest.

The Aztecs were almost always at war. Conquered cities would supply the tribute which made the Aztecs rich, and war provided a steady stream of victims for the sacrifices which the Aztecs believed were vital to their well-being.

NEGOTIATIONS
Once the Aztecs had decided to conquer a particular city, they sent ambassadors from Tenochtitlan to offer the city "protection." They pointed out – very politely – the advantages of being able to trade with the Empire. All they asked for was a small gift of gold or precious stones for the Emperor. The city was given twenty days to consider their request.

If the city refused, more ambassadors arrived. This time the talk was tougher, less about the advantages of joining the Aztecs than about the destruction and death which came to any city that did not submit.

To show how confident they were about the outcome of any future war, the Aztecs gave the enemy chief a magic potion to make him strong in battle and presents of weapons for his soldiers!

If this did not work, a third embassy arrived twenty days later. Polite talk was replaced by bloodcurdling threats about what would happen after the city lost the war. This included destruction of the city's temple, enslavement of most of the population, and a promise that crippling tribute would be demanded for years to come.

WAR!
If the city still refused to join the Aztecs, the war began. Messengers were dispatched to the cities throughout the Empire to gather soldiers for the war. On the day chosen by the priests as the luckiest day to start the campaign, the great war drum boomed out over Tenochtitlan and the army gathered in the Temple Precinct.

Eventually a huge force set out, complete with priests, women cooks, porters, and engineers. The soldiers from each city marched in separate groups. The army was fed by the cities through which it passed. Discipline was fierce, and soldiers who stole from or attacked a civilian were executed.

THE BATTLE
When the army arrived at the enemy city, Jaguar knights were sent to spy out the land. They signalled to each other by imitating bird calls. The Eagle knights attacked at dawn, making a great noise, stamping their feet, chanting, and whistling loudly to frighten the foe. Then the Jaguar knights encircled their enemy.

The fighting was very fierce, but the Aztecs tried to wound or capture their enemies rather than kill them. When the Aztec general decided that the battle was won, heralds were sent to call on their opponents to surrender.

Aztec officers were almost all nobles, although a few of them were commoners promoted because of their bravery in battle. They wore feathered standards in battle as symbols of their authority. Aztec battle plans were always carefully prepared using spies and maps made by travelling merchants.

Part of the story of a war. On the left, rebel soldiers attack Aztec pochteca, *providing the excuse for war. On the right the defeated rebel leader is told of his imminent execution.*

In battle, Aztec soldiers tried to take prisoners rather than kill their enemies. Warriors were graded and rewarded according to the number of prisoners they took in battle.

SURRENDER

Once the enemy surrendered, a peace treaty was drawn up which listed the amount of tribute the conquered city had to pay. Sometimes, a conquered city would be governed by an Aztec noble. Prisoners - men, women, and children - were taken back to the victorious cities until the time came for them to be sacrificed.

WAR OF FLOWERS

Occasionally there were periods when there was no war. At such times, the cities of the Triple Alliance would arrange to fight "Wars of Flowers" with certain neighbors, such as Tlaxcala, whose people were particularly valued as offerings. These battles were like ceremonial tournaments. When it was decided that each side had enough prisoners, the battle was ended and the armies returned home with their spoils.

TRADE AND TRIBUTE

This life-sized skull was carved from a solid piece of crystal using only stone tools. Skulls, which are powerful symbols of death, appear in many Aztec works of art.

Much of the wealth of the Aztecs came from tribute sent to Tenochtitlan by the other cities in the Empire. Gathering tribute was very well organized, with Aztec tax gatherers, called *calpixques*, stationed at key points throughout the Empire to supervise the system's operation.

GATHERING TRIBUTE

Every few months, lists of the tribute required from each city were sent out from the capital. If the cities refused to send the tribute, war was declared. Throughout the year, but especially at harvest time, a constant stream of goods was carried into Tenochtitlan to be stored in the city's warehouses.

MERCHANTS

The Aztecs also acquired the goods they needed by trade. The travelling merchants, called *pochteca*, led very different lives from those of other Aztecs. They lived in separate areas in the city and all belonged to a merchant guild. They had their own laws and judges and worshipped their own god, Yacatecuhtli - the "Lord Who Guides" or "Lord Nose" - to whom they made offerings so he would protect them on their journeys. The children of merchants were allowed to marry only the children of other merchants.

Merchants were afraid of being envied by the nobles, so they hid their great wealth, dressing in plain cloaks and headdresses made of cactus fiber.

Collecting tribute was the key to Aztec power. It provided the Aztecs with great wealth and kept the conquered cities under their control.

Officials kept detailed lists of the tribute sent from all conquered cities. This tribute list shows cloaks, shields, and a decorated suit of armor (top), jade beads (center left), 16,000 rubber balls (center right), bundles of feathers (bottom left) and 200 bags of cacao beans (bottom right).

SPYING

As well as adding to the great wealth of the Aztecs, the merchants were useful in other ways. Some acted as spies, reporting to Aztec generals about the wealth of other cities and the size of their armies. Sometimes they were told to cause trouble in an area which the Aztecs wanted to attack. They would find a way to insult a local chief so that their expedition would be attacked. The Aztec armies would then march in to restore order and make sure the trade routes were safe – and to collect prisoners for sacrifice.

HIDING THEIR WEALTH

The merchants always returned secretly, arriving at night with the goods in their canoes or packs, well covered. Everything was then hidden in the house of another trader. Merchants were always very careful to keep their enormous wealth and trade secrets hidden from other Aztecs.

TRADING EXPEDITIONS

The *pochteca* went on long trading journeys to all corners of the Empire. When preparing for an expedition, great care was taken. They chose a lucky date and cut their hair for the last time until they returned. Their departure was announced in the marketplace so that other people could join the trading expedition. The merchants left the Valley of Mexico carrying goods belonging to many different merchants, each of whom shared in the profits - or losses - of the venture. The *pochteca* were heavily armed and took large numbers of soldiers with them.

Since the Aztecs had no pack animals - they had never even seen horses or oxen - all their trade goods were carried by porters in bundles on their backs. They returned with luxury goods from all corners of the Empire, such as fine cloth, dyes, cacao beans, gold, cotton, feathers, jade beads, and copper.

Merchants returning to Tenochtitlan. Since the Aztecs had no pack animals and only used the wheel as a toy, all their trade goods had to be carried overland by porters. The heavy bundles were carried in wooden frames strapped to the porters' backs and supported with a strap around the forehead.

23

THE EMPEROR

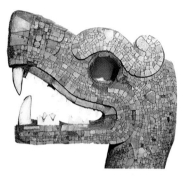

This double-headed serpent pendant was worn by the high priest of Tlaloc, the rain god. It is probably supposed to be a rattlesnake, which the Aztecs revered. It is carved in wood and covered with tiny mosaic tiles of turquoise and shell. Montezuma may have worn something similar.

When the Aztecs were a wandering group, their leader was elected by the senior members of the group. They always chose the person who would be the strongest leader. As the Aztecs grew more powerful, so their leader changed from being one of many tribal chiefs to being a powerful Emperor. His title was Tlatoani, which means "He Who Speaks."

THE ROYAL FAMILY

By 1519, although a council still elected the Emperor, he was always a member of the "royal family," usually the brother or sometimes the nephew of the last Emperor. Since the Aztec nobles were allowed to take several wives, there were usually plenty of suitable candidates. Many of the important positions in the Empire were held by the Emperor's relatives, so any new Emperor already had experience in government.

Unlike many European emperors and kings at the time, the Aztec leader did not claim to own all the land and the people in the Empire. The Aztecs were divided into clans, each with its own chieftain to make the day-to-day decisions. Nevertheless, the Emperor was extremely powerful. He was the high priest, the commander-in-chief of the army, overall ruler of the huge Empire, and a living god to his people.

The great Montezuma got down from his litter... and many more lords walked before him, sweeping the ground on which he was to tread, and laying down cloaks so that his feet should not touch the earth.

— Bernal Diaz —

PUBLIC APPEARANCES

The Emperor rarely appeared in public, and then only amidst great ceremony. People coming into the presence of the Emperor had to follow strict rules. Plain clothes replaced their usual rich cloaks, and they stood barefoot, bowing before the Emperor three times. An ordinary person was not even allowed to look directly at the Emperor's face.

MONTEZUMA

At the time of the Spanish conquest the Emperor was Montezuma II. When Montezuma became Emperor in 1502, he broke with earlier Aztec tradition, forcing all those not of noble birth to leave his palace. For the next 15 years, he was rarely in Tenochtitlan, but went away to war.

Whenever the Emperor appeared in public, he was carried through the streets on a litter by teams of important nobles.

A ROYAL PALACE

1 Reception chamber
2 Emperor's personal apartments
3 Emperor's tribute store
4 Garden courtyard
5 Emperor receiving tribute
6 Scribes writing tribute lists
7 Room lit by torches
8 Bundles of paper
9 Weapons store

Hidden treasure store

Montezuma's palace

The royal palace was surrounded by magnificent gardens and a wall, and lay next to the Temple Precinct. It was a two-story building with courtyards. While the furniture was very simple, many of the walls were covered with paintings, carvings, and gold panels. The rooms on the ground floor, which were used for government business, included a council chamber and law court; the royal treasury; a records room for tribute lists; living quarters for 3,000 servants and guards; a weapons store; guest rooms for visiting ambassadors; and, unknown to most people, a hidden treasure room. Montezuma and his family used the upper floors as living quarters.

WRITING

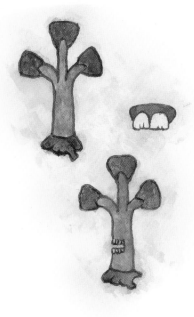

The glyph for the words tree *(top left) and* teeth *(top right) are put together to make the sound of Quauhtitlan (bottom).*

The Aztecs did not have an alphabet. Instead, they wrote in pictures, or glyphs. Some glyphs were simply pictures of objects, such as a tree or a knife. Other glyphs represented ideas. War, for example, was shown by a picture of a shield and a club. Speech was represented by small scrolls coming out of the mouth of the speaker. Motion was shown by a line of footprints. The glyphs were drawn first in black and then colored in.

SOUND SIGNS

Some glyphs came to represent the sound of the object they showed. These glyphs were called phonograms and could be put together to spell out the sound of a word. This method was often used for writing the names of places. For example, by combining the glyph for a tree (*quauitl*) with the glyph for teeth (*tlantli*), the scribe created a new glyph which sounded like the city of Quauhtitlan.

READING PICTURES

Glyphs were not written on a page in regular order. They were drawn to make a scene which had to be interpreted by the reader, in the same way that we might try to solve a picture puzzle. The position and size of the glyphs were important. Things which were supposed to be further away were drawn at the top of the page, with nearer things at the bottom. Glyphs which were more important would be drawn larger.

This type of picture writing is not easy to understand, nor is it easy to use. It is not surprising that only a few skilled scribes, usually priests, could read and write.

PAPER

Paper was made from the bark of wild fig trees, which was soaked in lime water and beaten to separate the fibers. The pulp was mixed with gum and beaten into thin sheets. The sheets were often stuck together to make a long concertina-like book called a codex. Some codices were painted on parchment made of animal skin.

An Aztec codex. Most early Mexican cultures had paper and writing, and made codices. Some codices tell stories from Mexican history. Others are religious almanacs containing weather forecasts and prophecies which named lucky and unlucky days for farming and fighting. These concertina-like books provide much information for historians studying Mexican civilization.

OFFICIAL PAPERWORK

Ruling the vast Aztec Empire required large numbers of written records dealing with tribute owed and collected, orders given to officials, and reports from other cities. In addition, each *calpulli* kept detailed maps, and records of the land held by its members. Every temple had a large library of religious and astrological books. Priests believed the stars and planets affected the lives of their people, and they kept records of eclipses, planetary events, and star movements. All this writing meant that a lot of paper was used, and nearly half a million sheets were sent as tribute each year.

COUNTING

The Aztecs were also able to write numbers. Their counting system was based on 20, the number of fingers and toes each person has. The numbers 1 to 19 were represented by fingers; the number 20 was shown by a flag; the number 400 (20 x 20) was a feather; and the number 8,000 (20 x 20 x 20) was a bag, which could hold that number of cacao beans.

1-19   **20**

400   **8,000**

441 cloaks

Numbers were represented by symbols. They can be seen on tribute lists, which showed precisely the amount of goods to be supplied to Tenochtitlan.

27

For important festivals, the Aztecs used small pottery stamps to make face-paint patterns on their cheeks.

Craftworkers were honored highly by the Aztecs. They lived in their own areas of the city, and had their own gods and festivals. They guarded the secrets of their trades jealously and passed on their skills only to their own children. They were called tolteca after the Toltecs who, according to legend, were their ancestors.

METALWORKERS

The Aztecs had no iron, but they used copper, gold, and silver to make jewelry. These metals came from the far reaches of the Empire, either as tribute or as trade goods acquired by the *pochteca*, the travelling merchants.

To make a metal object, the metalworker first made a clay model. This was covered with beeswax and then coated with more clay. A small furnace heated by charcoal was used to melt the metal. Air was blown into the embers of the fire through a metal tube, to make the fire hot enough. The molten metal was then poured into a hole in the top of the mold. The heat melted the wax, which was replaced by the metal. The mold was left to cool and then the clay was smashed to leave the finished metal object . Using this "lost-wax" method,

Aztec metalworkers were able to make very detailed and delicate objects, such as lip plugs for pierced lips, and tiny bells and pendants. Larger metal objects, such as wall panels or statues, were made by heating and hammering large lumps of metal. The most valuable objects were made of gold, but sometimes copper was added to the gold to make a very effective imitation. Most solid gold objects were melted down by the Spanish and only written descriptions of these items survived.

The Aztecs used wheels only as toys. Wheels for moving heavy objects were unknown, although without draft animals, carts might not have been very useful.

FEATHERWORK

Featherworkers had their own guild. They made many beautiful objects which have almost all been destroyed. The most highly prized feathers came from the brilliant plumage of the Quetzal bird. There was a huge aviary in Tenochtitlan where many thousands of brightly-colored birds were cared for by 300 workers. As the birds molted, the feathers were collected, graded, and taken to the featherworkers.

Feathers were used to make mosaic pictures. The design was drawn out on a piece of cloth and the feathers were glued in place to make the pattern. Feathers were also "woven" into magnificent banners, headdresses, and cloaks. This technique involved placing the feathers on a frame and sewing them into place.

Metalworkers often operated in pairs. One of them hammered and worked the gold, while the other kept the charcoal furnace hot by blowing on the embers through a tube.

Feathers were either gathered from captive birds, or bought in the market place, then dyed with bright colors.

The featherworker, who was a member of the feather-workers' guild, first drew the design on a piece of cloth.

The featherworker arranged the dyed feathers into the required pattern before glueing or sewing them into place.

OTHER CRAFTS

Other craftworkers produced fine statues, mosaics, and objects made of jade crystal, obsidian, and semi-precious stones such as turquoise. Delicate plates and bowls were made by skilled potters without using the potter's wheel, then unknown. Cloth-making, too, was important. Women wove all their own brightly colored clothes and cloaks using belt looms. Nobles wore cotton clothes, while those of ordinary people were made from cactus fiber.

MUSIC

The main musical instrument was the *huehuetl*, a drum made from a hollow log. This provided a strong bass rhythm. Higher sounds were provided by wooden gongs, rattles, bells, and other objects which tinkled and jangled, such as bones, dried seeds, and nuts. The only wind instruments the Aztecs had were conch shells, which were used to waken the citizens each day, and flutes made of bone, pottery, or bamboo. Music, singing, and dancing played an important part in almost all festivals and ceremonies. Royal musicians could be punished if their instruments were out of tune.

This magnificent headdress is decorated with Quetzal feathers. It was part of a ceremonial costume worn by priests impersonating a god. It is one of very few pieces of Aztec featherwork which still survives.

An ocarina and flute made from pottery. Aztec music was very rhythmical and was used to accompany dancing.

FOOD AND FARMING

A jug made of calcite carved in the shape of a hare. A vessel like this would have been used in a rich household to hold the drink cacao.

Most Aztecs were farmers who worked very hard from dawn to dusk in the fields. The Aztecs had no draft animals and no ploughs, so the land had to be dug by hand. The fields were very fertile, thanks to the rich lake mud and the human dung brought in boats from the city's public bathrooms.

THE CHINAMPAS

The best fields were the *chinampas*, or floating gardens. These fields were built by hammering posts into the bottom of Lake Texcoco. Bundles of reeds and branches weighted with stones were sunk between the poles to make a foundation. Wicker-work matting was attached to the posts, then piled high with mud dredged from the lake. Willow trees were planted round the edges of the *chinampas* so their roots would keep the fertile soil from washing away.

Houses for the farmers were built on the islands. A family farmed about six *chinampas*, each of which was roughly 100 yards (meters) long by 10 yards (meters) wide.

FOOD

Ordinary Aztecs, in spite of their active lives, ate surprisingly little food. Because they had no large domestic animals, such as cattle, meat was a luxury. But they ate quite a wide variety of fruits and vegetables, such as sweet potatoes, tomatoes, and avocados. They also ate peanuts and squash.

The staple diet of the Aztecs was maize and vegetables. They ate little meat and liked their food hot and spicy.

MAIZE

The staple food was maize. The dried cobs could be stored almost indefinitely, which was a big advantage in a country where the land and weather made the harvest unpredictable. The maize flour was used to make thin cakes called *tortillas*. These soon went stale, so they were made fresh for each meal. A child of three would eat half a *tortilla* per day; a child of 13, two per day.

Maize was stored in large corn bins made of stone and clay. The top of the bin was wider than the base to stop rats climbing up the sides. Overhanging thatched roofs stopped the rain soaking the cobs. Notice the notched tree trunk used as a ladder.

The maize was also used to make *atole*, a sort of porridge, which was flavored with peppers or sweetened with honey. It was also made into *tamales*, which were envelopes of steamed maize usually stuffed with vegetables or other fillings. Common fillings used by the Aztecs were beans, egg, peppers, fish, and fruit. Other fillings, which were thought to be great delicacies, included frogs, newts, snails, insect eggs, boiled grasshoppers, and the red worms which lived in the mud of Lake Texcoco.

MEAT

Some meat was obtained by hunting – waterfowl, deer, wild pig, rabbits, and gophers. Turkeys were kept for their meat and eggs. But one of the greatest delicacies the Aztecs enjoyed was dog. Most families raised and fattened small hairless dogs for special feasts.

LUXURY FOOD

Richer Aztecs ate very well and frequently attended elaborate feasts. They dined on such luxuries as pineapples brought from the hot lands to the south, crab, oysters, turtle, and seafish from the coast. Chocolate, made from crushed *cacao* nuts, was whipped up into a cold, frothy drink flavored with vanilla or spices. Fifty large jugs of this delicious drink were prepared for the royal household every day.

DRINK

The poor drank water except during certain festivals when they were allowed to drink *pulque*, a kind of beer made from the sap of a cactus plant. They drank sparingly, for drunkenness was a crime which could be punished by death.

MEAL TIMES

Aztec farmers generally started work at dawn. They worked for several hours before having their breakfast of *atole* at about 10 o'clock. If they were working far from their homes they would make do with a cold snack. They ate their main meal of *tortillas* and spicy filling during the hottest part of the day, and then took a siesta before going back to work. They often ate another bowl of porridge before going to bed.

Every Aztec home had its comal, a circular clay griddle supported by three stones, on which tortillas were cooked.

The fertile chinampas were regularly maintained, manured with human dung, and dug with pointed digging sticks.

HOMES

Aztec pottery was very delicate, although it was made by hand shaping and not thrown on a potter's wheel.

Rich nobles lived in large two-story houses surrounded by a garden enclosed by a high wall. The walls were made of stone or adobe (mud bricks covered with plaster). Most houses had flat roofs, some with gardens on them. The houses were generally built in the shape of a hollow square with a courtyard in the middle. The outside walls were blank and feature-less. The rooms which opened on to the courtyard were large and airy, often with large pillars as decoration.

INTERNAL LAYOUT

Inside there was a dining room, a reception room, sleeping rooms, a kitchen, servants' quarters, and even a punishment room. The floors were made of cement or polished stone. The outside doors were usually wooden, while the inside doorways were filled with cloth curtains or hanging mats. The Aztecs had no locks so they sewed small bells to the curtains to warn them of intruders.

The courtyards of houses belonging to Aztec nobles often contained colorful gardens and cooling fountains.

The walls of every Aztec house contained niches in which stood small statues of gods. Each family made regular sacrifices of food and animals at these household shrines.

STEAM BATH

The Aztecs loved to keep clean. The Emperor Montezuma washed twice a day, and ordinary Aztecs bathed regularly in lakes and rivers using the roots of certain plants as soap. Many houses had small steam baths built beside them. These baths were often shaped like igloos and were similar to our modern saunas. A fire was lit in the fireplace outside. This heated the walls of the steam bath until they glowed red-hot. The bather went inside and threw water on the hot walls until the tiny room filled with steam. The heat opened the pores in the bather's skin and the sweat was rubbed off with twigs or grass.

HOUSES OF ORDINARY PEOPLE

Poorer people lived in much simpler houses mostly built of adobe or wattle and daub, which was often brightly painted. By law these houses could only be one story high, usually with a flat roof covered with wooden tiles, or a pitched, thatched roof. There were seldom more than two rooms, one for living and eating, and the other for sleeping. The house had one entrance door and no windows.

A SIMPLE HOUSE

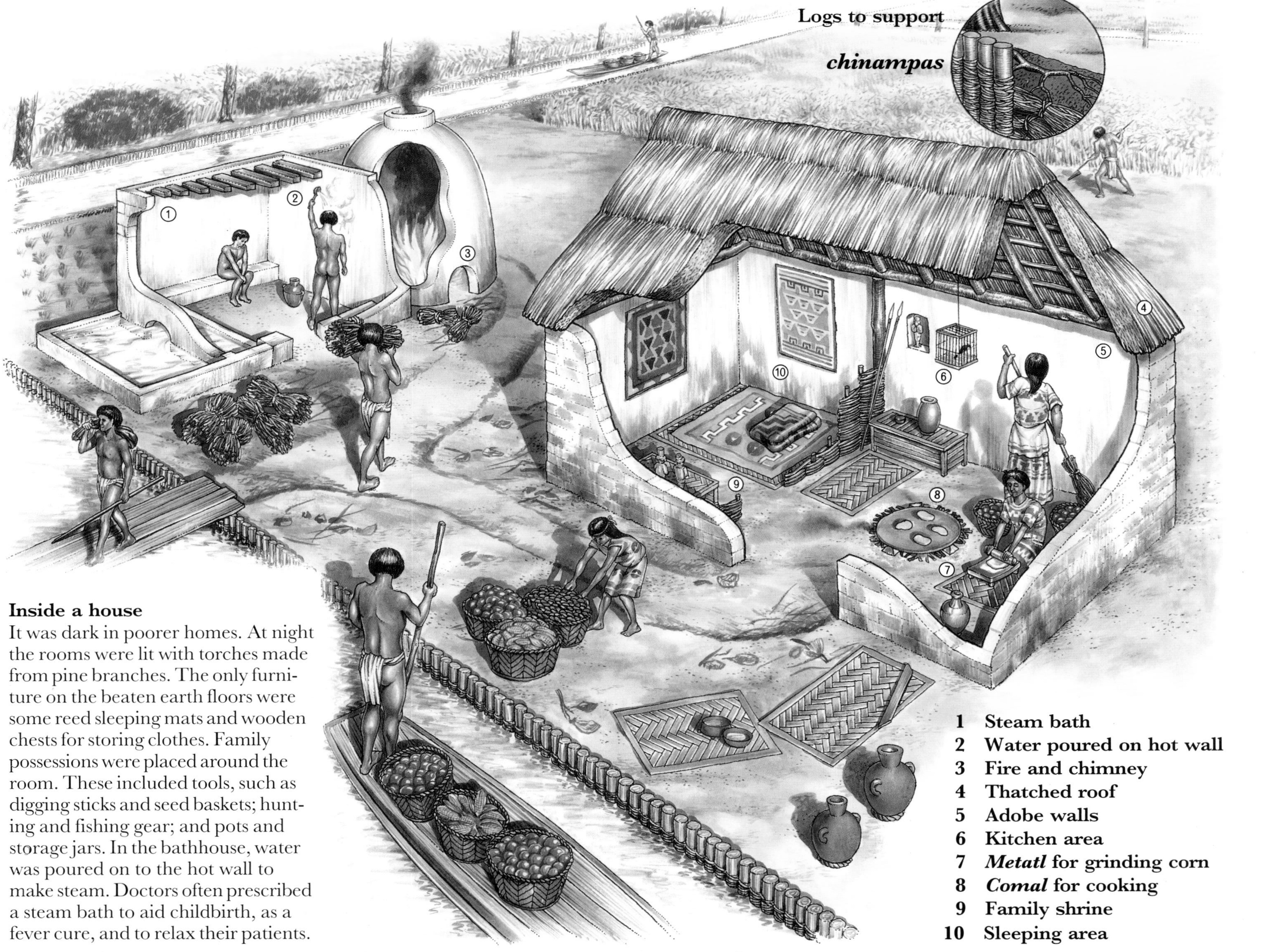

Logs to support
chinampas

1 Steam bath
2 Water poured on hot wall
3 Fire and chimney
4 Thatched roof
5 Adobe walls
6 Kitchen area
7 *Metatl* for grinding corn
8 *Comal* for cooking
9 Family shrine
10 Sleeping area

Inside a house

It was dark in poorer homes. At night the rooms were lit with torches made from pine branches. The only furniture on the beaten earth floors were some reed sleeping mats and wooden chests for storing clothes. Family possessions were placed around the room. These included tools, such as digging sticks and seed baskets; hunting and fishing gear; and pots and storage jars. In the bathhouse, water was poured on to the hot wall to make steam. Doctors often prescribed a steam bath to aid childbirth, as a fever cure, and to relax their patients.

GROWING UP

An Aztec midwife and a newborn baby. The midwife ceremonially washed the baby and then named it.

The game of patolli *was very popular. The game was a combination of ludo and backgammon. Beans were used as counters, and adult players bet heavily on the outcome.*

The birth of a child was a cause for great celebration. The moment a baby arrived, the parents called in an astrologer to decide what would be a lucky day to name the child. Children often took the day of their birth as part of their own name. The other part of their name might have something to do with animals or objects or characteristics.

NAMES

In this way Aztecs were given names such as Angry Eagle One Wind, or He Who Laughs Loudly Four Earthquake. Girls were given more attractive names, such as Green Jade or Rain Bird, flower names being especially popular. Some of these names were quite a mouthful, such as the girl's name Tziquetzalpoztectsin, which meant "Quetzal Bird," a bird highly prized for its beautiful plumage.

From the age of about three, children were taught skills which would help them in later life. Every child helped with jobs around the house, and was taught the virtues of good manners, hard work, and dignified behavior.

EDUCATION OF GIRLS

Women were not considered very important in the warrior society of the Aztecs. Their main purpose in life was to bear children. Young girls were, therefore, taught all the skills they would need as housewives. This included cooking, spinning, and weaving. By the time a girl married at the age of 16, she was an expert in all household skills. Some daughters of rich families were sent to a temple or school to be trained as priestesses.

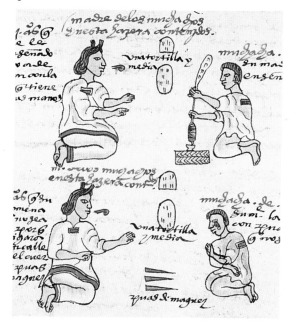

Codices tell us much about the small details of Aztec life. In this one, a girl is taught to spin cotton with a spindle (top). However, when she is disobedient (bottom), her parent threatens her with the maguey cactus thorns which lie between them. Note the speech glyph, and the dark patch on the child's cheek which represents tears.

EDUCATION OF BOYS

Boys were taught the skills of fishing and farming. Most of their early education came from their father, then at the age of five they went to school. Children who misbehaved were treated very severely. They were pricked with sharp thorns, beaten, tied up and laid in a patch of mud, or given extra jobs to do.

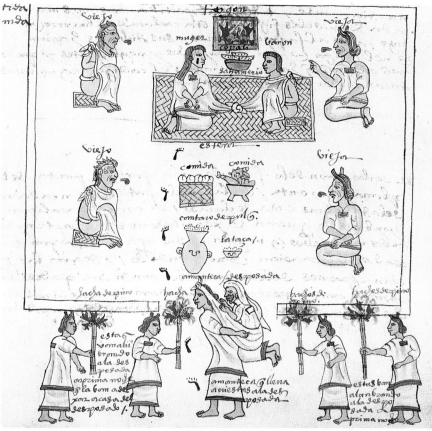

Aztecs wanted their children to have a "stone face and a stone heart". Angry parents used a whole range of vicious punishments - including holding them over a fire with hot peppers on it - to train unruly or disobedient children.

SCHOOLS

The children of ordinary Aztecs went to a clan school called a *telpochcalli*, or "House of Youth," to learn how to be good citizens. The education was free and they learned history, religion, music, and dancing. The boys also did a great deal of hard work digging ditches and carrying water to toughen themselves. They were taught how to handle weapons and took part in mock battles to learn the skills of a warrior. Young boys often acted as servants with the Aztec army and watched how war was conducted.

The children of nobles went to a school called a *calmecac*. Their education was very different from that of ordinary Aztec children and was designed to turn them into priests, generals, judges, and government officials. They learned mathematics, astrology, law, reading, writing, and how to use the calendar. Discipline was very strict. There were also *calmecac* schools for girls where they spent much of their time in silence, and had many lessons about religion.

Girls married at about the age of 16. During the wedding ceremony, the older women carried the bride to the groom's house on their backs and tied the couple's cloaks together to seal the marriage.

Aztec education was not all unrelieved horror! Learning how to dance and play music were important social skills and some of the more enjoyable school lessons.

THE CALENDAR

Understanding time was crucial to the Aztecs. They needed to know practical things such as when to plant and when to harvest. Much more importantly, these superstitious people wanted to know which days were lucky and which unlucky.

THE SOLAR CALENDAR

The Aztecs had two calendars. One of these, the solar calendar, was very like ours. A year was divided into 18 "months", each of which had 20 days. (Like their counting system, their calendar was based on the number 20, the total of one person's toes and fingers.) This gave a total of only 360 days. The remaining five days were thought to be very unlucky - it was believed that arguments started during the "nothing" days could last for ever, and that children born then would never amount to anything. During this time the Aztecs

The great Aztec calendar stone. Used to predict eclipses, it was originally painted in vivid colors, and shows the glyphs of all the days of the Aztec year.

stayed indoors and did nothing. At the start of each 20-day "month" the Aztecs wore their best clothes and took part in dancing and singing, while sacrifices of humans, animals, and fruit were made according to the time of year. The months had names which reflected the seasons, such as "Drought," "Fall of the Fruits," "Month of Sweeping," and "Growth."

THE SACRED CALENDAR

The other calendar was the sacred calendar, Tonalphoualli (the "Count of Days"), which was important for the priests and astrologers. This calendar was used mainly for making prophecies and deciding which days were lucky. The calendar is best shown as two interlocking cog wheels.

The left-hand wheel has 13 numbers. The right-hand wheel has 20 named days. The wheels turn so that each number fits into a named day. The cycle starts on 1 Crocodile. The next day is 2 Wind, the third 3 House and so on. The wheels keep turning until the cycle returns to 1 Crocodile, by which time 260 days will have passed.

Certain days were thought to be especially lucky or unlucky, and each day had its own god. Quetzalcoatl was the wind god and so was lord of the sign Wind. The priests used the numbers, the named days, and certain colors and directions which were associated with them, to make divinations and cast horoscopes.

THE BUNDLE OF YEARS

The solar calendar and the sacred calendar worked together. The first day of each calendar occurred at the same time only once every 52 years. This was considered a period of terrible danger when the world could come to an end. No one was sure if the sun would rise again at the end of this Xiuhmolpilli, or "Bundle of Years".

The "nothing" days at the end of the 52-year period lasted for 12 days. This was because the extra days in what we call leap years were all added together and put at the end of the Bundle of Years. During these 12 days, people threw away all their old clothes, smashed their pots and extinguished all fires. People stayed indoors and men stayed away from their families, fearing that the women would turn into beasts and eat them!

THE NEW CENTURY

On the last night of the "nothing days," priests, dressed as the chief gods, waited high on an extinct volcano called the "Hill of the Star." When the Evening Star reached the center of the sky, the priests stretched a captive over an altar. The high priest lit a fire on a piece of wood on the victim's chest and tore out his heart. From this flame, torches were lighted and carried throughout the countryside to kindle sacred temple fires. Thus the world was made safe for the next 52 years.

A representation of the sacred calendar, showing 1 Rabbit. The smaller wheel shows the numbers 1-13. The larger wheel shows the 20 named days.

The "New Fire" ceremony was extremely dramatic, with some of the priests dressed as gods. The victim always came from a noble family.

37

WORSHIP OF THE GODS

A stone mask of the god Quetzalcoatl, the "Plumed Serpent", god of the wind and of writing.

The Aztecs had many gods, who they believed controlled everything in the world, and whose anger could only be stilled by the correct ceremonies at the right times. In worshipping their gods, the Aztecs were not trying to lead better lives; they were trying to win the favor of the gods by their offerings and sacrifices. When disasters occurred, such as earthquakes or droughts, the Aztecs knew the gods were angry and so made greater efforts to please them.

THE WORK OF THE PRIESTS

There were tens of thousands of priests, priestesses, and astrologers in the Aztec Empire. About 5,000 worked at the temple of Huitzilopochtli alone. They were very important people in Aztec society and were treated as nobles. There were many ranks of priests, with the High Priests of Tlaloc and Huitzilopochtli at the top, and young trainees at the bottom.

TRAINING TO BE A PRIEST

Boys started to train as priests when they went to *calmecac*. They had to learn to read and write so they could interpret the sacred calendars and religious codices. They also learned the skills of divination and prophecy, so they were able to foretell important events such as eclipses, droughts, and floods. They memorized the correct prayers and religious songs for each of the gods.

An incense burner shaped like a "turkey claw" - one of the many names of the "Smoking Mirror" god, Tezcatlipoca.

At night, senior priests went to the mountains to give blood to the gods. Each carried an incense burner, an incense bag decorated with three tassels, and a tobacco bag.

THE LIFE OF A PRIEST

Priests led very uncomfortable lives. They had to pray and make offerings in the temple every few hours, and make sure that the sacred fires were kept lit. They fasted regularly and had to give offerings of their own blood by pricking their tongues, ears, and limbs with sharp thorns. They had to take part in dozens of important ceremonies which were held throughout the year.

The most important priests were also astronomers. They observed the movement of the stars using a cross-shaped piece of wood, and from their calculations made predictions about the future. Most priests worked at temples. Their main job was to organize and participate in ceremonies. As part of this they performed human sacrifices. Other priests led less religious lives as teachers, warriors, and judges.

HUMAN SACRIFICE

The Aztecs believed that regular offerings of human blood and hearts were the only sure way to keep the sun moving. Human sacrifices were double offerings to the sun and mother earth to encourage them to provide food for humans. Sacrificial victims were held by the priests face upwards on the sacrificial stone while another priest cut open the captive's chest and tore out the heart. The heart was held up to the sun and then put into a sacred dish. The bodies were rolled down the temple steps where they lay in heaps. In some sacrifices the limbs and head were cut off, and the heads mounted on skull racks. Most of the victims went happily to their deaths, sure that they were going straight to the highest heaven.

Aztec priests observed the movements of the stars and planets with an instrument which was very similar to the cross-staff used by European navigators at the time.

A little apart... stood another small tower which was also an idol house of true hell, for one of its doors was in the shape of a terrible mouth, such as they paint to depict the jaws of hell. This mouth was open and contained great fangs to devour souls.

— Bernal Diaz —

HEAVEN AND HELL

The Aztecs believed the world was flat. Above the earth there were 13 heavens and below it there were nine hells. When people died, their souls wandered, suffering all kinds of trials, including the "Wind of Knives" which stripped the flesh from their bones. Eventually the dead reached the heaven or hell which was most suitable for them. Babies who died very young went to the "Heaven of the Milk Tree." People who drowned went to the "Heaven of Rain," a place full of rainbows. Men who died in battle, women who died in child-birth, and all sacrificial victims received the greatest honor, going to the heaven nearest the sun, the highest of all.

This Aztec picture, which is read from left to right, shows a priest being rewarded for bravery in battle. His costume becomes more elaborate as each new set of prisoners is taken.

THE FAMILY OF GODS

In ritual gladiatorial contests dedicated to Xipe Totec, four Eagle knights fought a victim who was tied to a heavy ceremonial stone, and armed with a mock sword with feather "blades."

Tlaloc, god of rain, was one of the most important Aztec deities. He could bring drought and famine. His shrine was built in a place of honor on the Great Temple at Tenochtitlan.

Among the most important Aztec gods were Xipe Totec, the "Flayed God," who was usually shown wearing a suit made of skin stripped from a sacrificed victim; Coatlicue, "Skirt of Serpents," the Earth goddess and mother of Huitzilopochtli, as well as 400 other sons; and Mictlantecuhtli, the fearsome god of death.

At first sight it seems as if the Aztecs had hundreds of gods. In fact most of the gods had several different names and controlled different things depending on the time of year, and where that particular god was being worshipped. Even so, the list of Aztec gods is extremely long and we may never fully understand the complex religion these people followed.

THE CHIEF GODS

The Aztecs borrowed most of their gods from the people who had come before them, such as the Olmecs and Toltecs. The most ancient gods were "Two Lord" and "Two Lady." Their four sons in turn created all the other gods, the world, and the human race. The four sons were all called Tezcatlipoca, which means "Smoking Mirror." They were: Red Tezcatlipoca, who was also called Xipe Totec, which means "Flayed God"; Blue Tezcatlipoca, also called Huitzilopochtli, which means "Blue Hummingbird" (sometimes "Left-Handed Hummingbird"), who was the tribal god of the Aztecs; White Tezcatlipoca, also called Quetzalcoatl, which means "Plumed Serpent"; and Black Tezcatlipoca, the "Lord of the Night Sky." Each god was also associated, among other things, with a direction, a color, a season, a day, a month, certain natural forces or events, and particular types of human behavior.

LEGENDS OF THE GODS

Many legends arose about the Aztec gods. Quetzalcoatl and Black Tezcatlipoca, for example, were believed to be locked in an everlasting battle to control the universe. They had already destroyed the universe four times, and four times the gods had rebuilt it.

The Aztecs were therefore living in the fifth universe, its people the creation of Quetzalcoatl. He had smashed up the bones of the dead and sprinkled them with his own blood to give them life. The pieces of bone were different shapes and sizes which explained why people did not look the same.

OTHER GODS

The four main gods created many other gods who each controlled at least one force of nature or type of human behavior, such as Ixtilton, the god of peaceful sleep, and Tlazolteotl, goddess of filth. There were also many lesser gods who were worshipped in different parts of the Empire, including dozens of maize gods and even several gods of the drink *pulque*.

THE TEMPLES AT MALINALCO

1 Jaguar knight statue
2 Serpent mouth entrance
3 Eagle knight statue
4 Inner sanctuary
5 Eagle altar
6 Temple hollowed from rock
7 Frieze of warriors
8 Packed earth roof
9 Firepit for burning offerings

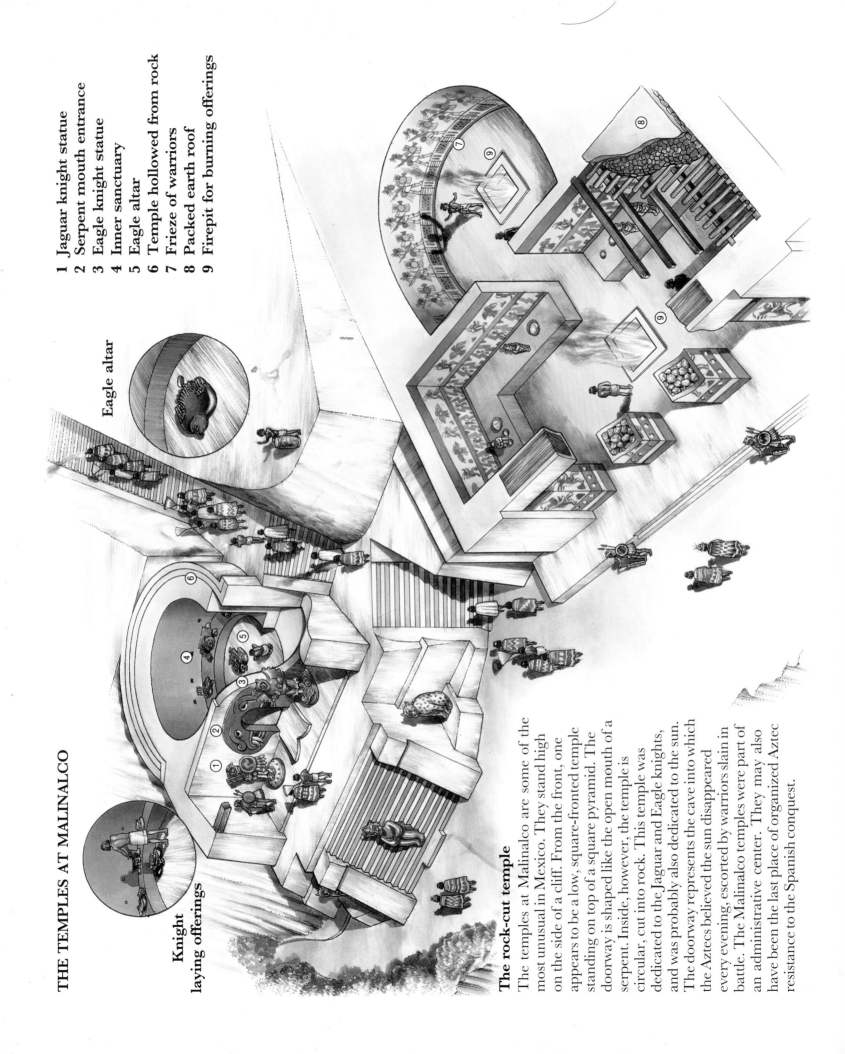

Eagle altar

Knight
laying offerings

The rock-cut temple

The temples at Malinalco are some of the most unusual in Mexico. They stand high on the side of a cliff. From the front, one appears to be a low, square-fronted temple standing on top of a square pyramid. The doorway is shaped like the open mouth of a serpent. Inside, however, the temple is circular, cut into rock. This temple was dedicated to the Jaguar and Eagle knights, and was probably also dedicated to the sun. The doorway represents the cave into which the Aztecs believed the sun disappeared every evening, escorted by warriors slain in battle. The Malinalco temples were part of an administrative center. They may also have been the last place of organized Aztec resistance to the Spanish conquest.

The Aztec glyph for One Reed, the year in which, according to Aztec legends, Quetzalcoatl would return.

In 1519, a Spanish soldier called Hernan Cortes was appointed by the Governor of Cuba to lead an expedition to the as-yet unexplored American mainland. Cortes and his band of about 500 men, most of whom were unemployed soldiers and were now looking to make their fortune, landed in Mexico.

THE LEGEND OF QUETZALCOATL

By the most amazing coincidence, 1519 was One Reed, the end of the Aztec 52-year cycle. It was a time when Aztec legends told that their god Quetzalcoatl would return from the east to destroy the Empire. As if to confirm the legend, several terrible events had happened in Tenochtitlan which were interpreted as bad omens. A comet had appeared in the sky; the temple of Huitzilopochtli had burst into flames; and, strangest of all, some fishermen were said to have caught an unusual ash-colored bird which had a mirror in its head. In this magic mirror, Montezuma said he saw strange soldiers riding four-legged monsters, destroying his Empire.

The peasant who brought news of huge "canoes" was imprisoned by Montezuma, who at first thought his story was an unbelievable lie!

HATRED OF THE AZTECS

The priests had demanded thousands of sacrifices from the cities of the Empire to counteract these evil omens. The resulting bloodbath sickened even those cities which had been friendly to the Aztecs. Never in their history had the Aztecs been so hated. When news reached Montezuma that strangers had landed, he was thrown into panic. He believed that Cortes must be the returning Quetzalcoatl. The reports he received about the Spanish made him even more fearful. The strangers were obviously very different from the Aztecs. They had white faces and yellow beards, just as Quetzalcoatl was supposed to have. They travelled in "canoes" as big as mountains. They also had many "magical" weapons, such as their cannons which spat fire and could split trees and mountains. The strangers dressed entirely in shining metal and rode strange four-footed beasts, the like of which the Aztecs had never seen.

MONTEZUMA'S DILEMMA

Montezuma hardly knew what to do. On the one hand these strangers might be human invaders who had come to loot the Empire. If that were the case, Montezuma should destroy them. On the other hand they might be gods. If the Aztecs attacked them, the gods might be so angry that they would destroy the Empire. Montezuma trembled with indecision.

An Aztec picture of the comet seen over Tenochtitlan in One Reed. Some astrologers tried to soothe Montezuma by saying it had never appeared! Others foretold terrible disasters.

THE AZTECS ATTACK

Montezuma decided to send presents to Cortes, and warned him not to approach Tenochtitlan, but this just made Cortes more determined to reach the legendary city. Montezuma ordered soldiers in the city of Cholula to attack the Spanish, but they were utterly defeated. The Spanish had stout armor, steel weapons, and guns. They were hard to kill and, more important, almost impossible to capture for sacrifice, which was the main aim of Aztec warfare.

Montezuma's plan to ambush the Spanish at Cholula went badly wrong and 6,000 of his soldiers were killed.

MEXICAN ALLIES

The Tlaxcalans, bitter enemies of the Aztecs, were very impressed by Cortes' ruthlessness, single-mindedness, and obvious military skill. They decided to join his small but powerful force in the hope that he would destroy the hated Aztecs. As a result, whenever Cortes fought a battle, it was with thousands of Mexican allies, as well as his own tough soldiers.

Montezuma showed Cortes around the city, but the two men distrusted each other. Cortes was disgusted by the Aztec religion, and Montezuma feared the Spanish soldiers.

THE MARCH ON TENOCHTITLAN

Cortes marched towards the capital, gathering allies as he went. When he reached Tenochtitlan, he and his troops were astounded by the size and beauty of the city. Montezuma came to meet the Spanish, still not sure if the strangers were humans or gods. By the time he realized the truth, it was already too late for him to save his people.

The Spanish were disciplined and experienced soldiers. The Aztecs had never seen horses before and were unable to deal with the weight and speed of Cortes' cavalry.

THE END OF THE EMPIRE

Montezuma greeted Cortes and his men as friends. For six days they toured Tenochtitlan, admiring its wonders. Then the mood began to change. The Spanish discovered a bricked-up doorway in the palace where they were living. In a moment of boredom they tore it down. Behind it they found several rooms heaped with jewels, silver, and gold. Here were the riches they had come to find!

In the final campaign, the Spanish and their Tlaxcalan allies advance along the causeway towards Tenochtitlan. Aztec warriors defend the city and attack the invaders from canoes. Cortes and Marina, his Indian interpreter, are shown in a Spanish ship.

HOSTAGE!

Shortly after this discovery, hearing that the Aztecs had killed two Spanish messengers, Cortes decided to seize Montezuma as a hostage. Cortes began to smash statues of Aztec gods and ordered Montezuma to put an end to human sacrifices. The Aztecs were horrified when Cortes had a chief burned alive for killing the messengers.

Then came news that another Spanish expedition had landed on the coast and was coming to arrest Cortes. The Spanish leader left the city with some of his troops to counter the threat. In his absence the Spanish who had been left behind tried to stop an important Aztec ceremony and were attacked. When Cortes returned, he found his men besieged in their palace. Cortes sent Montezuma to calm his people, but in the confusion, the Emperor was killed, stoned to death by his own people.

FLIGHT FROM TENOCHTITLAN

Cortes realized that the only way out of the city was at night. But as they crept away, the Spanish were attacked by a huge Aztec army, their escape slowed down by the destruction of the bridges on the causeways. Many Spanish soldiers drowned in the lake, weighed down by the huge amounts of treasure they were carrying.

teçiquauhtitlã

CORTES RETURNS

In the retreat, Cortes lost half his men and thousands of his Mexican allies. Eventually he reached the coast where he gathered reinforcements and launched a ferocious war on Aztec cities, destroying several armies sent against him. His own force now numbered nearly 1,000 Spanish and over 150,000 Mexicans. He decided to march against Tenochtitlan.

When Cortes reached Lake Texcoco he built ships, which he armed with cannons. Then his force sailed over the lake to attack the Aztec capital. It was a horrible battle. The Aztecs fought desperately, contesting every inch of the corpse-choked streets and canals. Spanish soldiers who were captured were sacrificed immediately. From their position on the outskirts of the city, the other Spanish could only watch in horror as their captured comrades were taken to the top of the Great Temple and sacrificed to appease the gods.

THE END OF THE AZTECS

Eventually the Aztecs could hold out no longer. The Spanish fought their way into the city center and slaughtered the inhabitants. With the fall of Tenochtitlan, virtually all Aztec resistance ended.

Cortes was appointed Governor of New Spain, the land previously ruled by the Aztecs, but a few years later was replaced. He returned to Spain where he was ignored by the king. Cortes died in 1547, unhappy and bitter.

After the death of Montezuma, Cortes believed he could escape secretly from Tenochtitlan, but the Spanish, heavily laden with booty, were ambushed. Their retreat cost them many dead. They called it La Noche Triste, *the Night of Sadness.*

AFTER THE CONQUEST

Spanish priests were sent to Mexico, and many Roman Catholic churches were built. The temples and buildings of Tenochtitlan were torn down, and the Aztecs' religion outlawed. The Aztecs, ravaged by European diseases such as smallpox, against which they had no immunity, could not stop the looting of their Empire. All the treasure the Spanish could find was sent back to Spain. In spite of the efforts of the Spanish priests, the Aztecs became slaves, working for their conquerors. Within 50 years almost no trace of the enormous, powerful, Aztec Empire remained.

The "dogging" of Mexicans. This Aztec picture dramatically shows the violent oppression they suffered after the conquest.

45

KEY DATES AND GLOSSARY

The Aztec Empire began at about the same time as the Renaissance in Europe, and ended just 29 years after Christopher Columbus made his famous voyage to the West Indies in 1492. Some of the earlier dates are approximate because of the problems of matching the Aztec calendar to our own.

1111 The Mexica leave Aztlan
1168 Fall of Toltec captial of Tula
1250 The Aztecs reach the Valley of Mexico (approximate)
1345 Foundation of Tenochtitlan
1358 Foundation of Tlatelolco
1417 Chimalpopoca becomes Emperor
1426 Itzcoatl becomes Emperor
1428 Aztecs overthrow the Tepanecs
1440 Montezuma I becomes Emperor
1446 Four-year war against Chalco begins
1450 The four-year great famine begins
1468 Axayacatl becomes Emperor
1481 Tizoc becomes Emperor
1486 Ahuitzotl becomes Emperor
1492 Columbus discovers the West Indies
1500 The flooding of Tenochtitlan
1502 Montezuma II becomes Emperor

1504 War against Tlaxcala begins
1511 The Spanish capture Cuba
1519 Cortes sets out for Mexico, 10 February
1519 Cortes enters Tenochtitlan, 8 November
1520 Death of Montezuma II, 27 June. Cuitlahuac becomes Emperor. Soon after Cuauhtemoc becomes Emperor
1520 Cortes abandons Tenochtitlan 1521. Final siege begins 28 April
1521 Fall of Tenochtitlan 13 August

Some pronunciations

e = *ay*
hui = *wee*
ll = *y*
u = *oo*
x = *h*
calpullec   *kal-pul-lek*
Huitzilopochtli   *wee-tseel-o-potch-tlee*
Mexicas   *May-hee-kahs*
Mixtecs   *mee-steks*
Nahuatl   *nah-wahtl*
pochteca   *potch-tay-kah*
tecuhtli   *tay-koo-tlee*
Tenochtitlan   *te-notch-ti-tlahn*
tortillas   *tor-tee-yas*

Glossary

adobe: mud bricks
atlatl: an Aztec spear thrower
atole: maize porridge
cacao: chocolate
calmecac: a school for the children of nobles
calpixque: a tax collector
calpulli: Aztec clans, the members of which were all related
chinampa: an artificial field built on a lake
Cihuacoatl: the Emperor's chief advisor
codex: an Aztec book made by glueing sheets of paper together in a concertina-like pattern.
comal: a circular griddle on which food was cooked
glyphs: picture writing
huehuetl: an Aztec drum
maceualtin: the common people, who were full citizens of the Empire
maguey: a variety of cactus which provided cloth and food for the Aztecs
maquahuitl: an Aztec sword made of wood into which were fixed a series of obsidian blades
metatl: an Aztec grindstone consisting of a ribbed stone "rolling pin" and a large curved stone
Nahuatl: the Aztec language
obsidian: a dark volcanic glass, used for weapon blades and other craft work
pochteca: Aztec merchants
pulque: beer made from cactus
tamale: a thin pancake of maize folded over to hold various edible fillings
teccalco: a lawcourt which tried serious cases in Tenochtitlan
tecuhtlis: the lesser Aztec nobles
telpochcalli: a school for members of the same clan
tlacochcalco: the main arms store in Tencochtitlan
Tlaxcala: a Mexican city which was the main enemy of the Aztecs
tlatoani: the highest Aztec nobles
tolteca: craftworkers
Tonalphoualli: the Aztec sacred calendar
tortilla: a thin maize cake
tribute: goods which had been given to the Aztec Emperor by conquered cities
Xiuhmolpilli: the "nothing days" at the end of a 52-year cycle

The quotations

Most of the quotations from this book are taken from the memoirs of a Spanish soldier, Bernal Diaz (*The Conquest of New Spain*, translated in the Penguin Classics series published in 1963). Diaz, who was born in 1492, was the longest-lived of Cortes' companions. He died, penniless, at the age of 89. He did not begin his eyewitness account of Cortes' expedition until he was over 70. Even so, his account is both vigorous and detailed. The Aztec poems are taken from the 100 or so which were written down by Roman Catholic priests shortly after the conquest.

INDEX

48

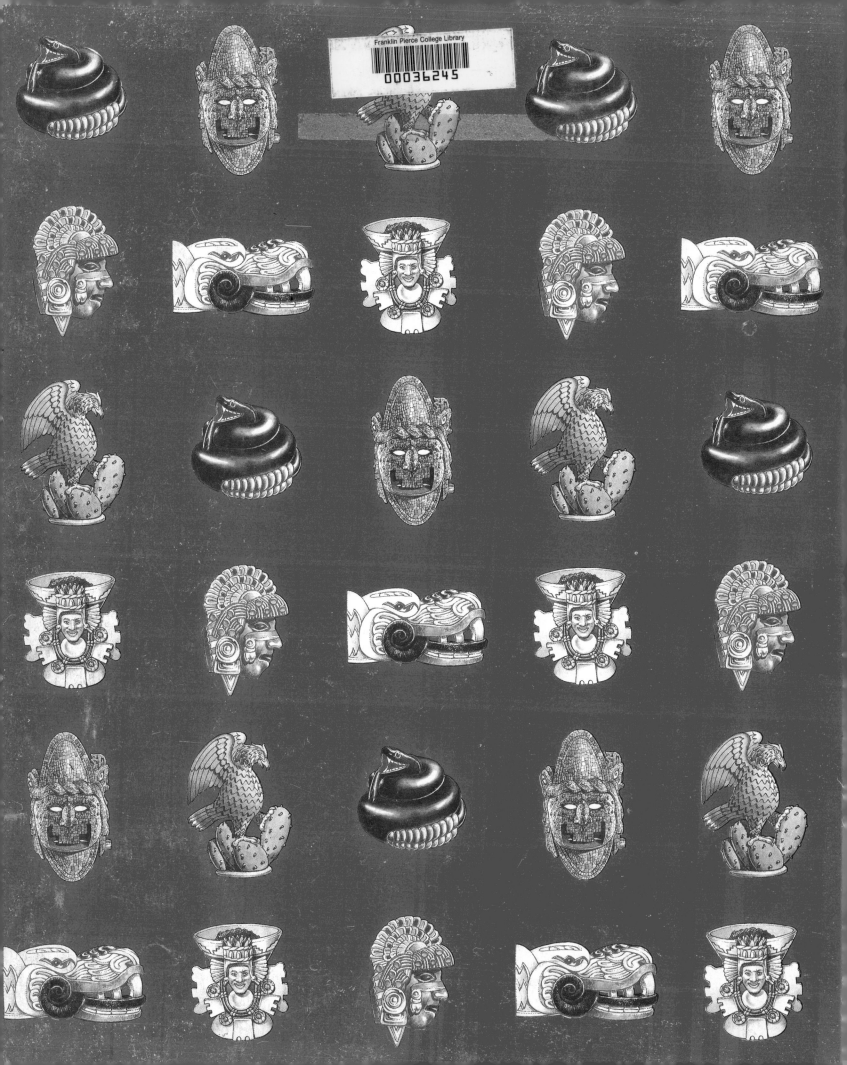